Beginning-to-Read
Riddles and Jokes

Alice Thompson Gilbreath
illustrated by Susan Perl

Follett Publishing Company

Chicago **F** New York

Copyright © 1967, by Follett Publishing Company. All rights reserved. No part of this book may be reproduced in any form without written permission from the publisher. Manufactured in the United States of America. Published simultaneously in Canada by The Ryerson Press, Toronto.

Library of Congress Catalog Card Number: 67-21164

SBN 695-47740-4 Titan binding   SBN 695-87740-2 Trade binding   Second Printing

RIDDLES

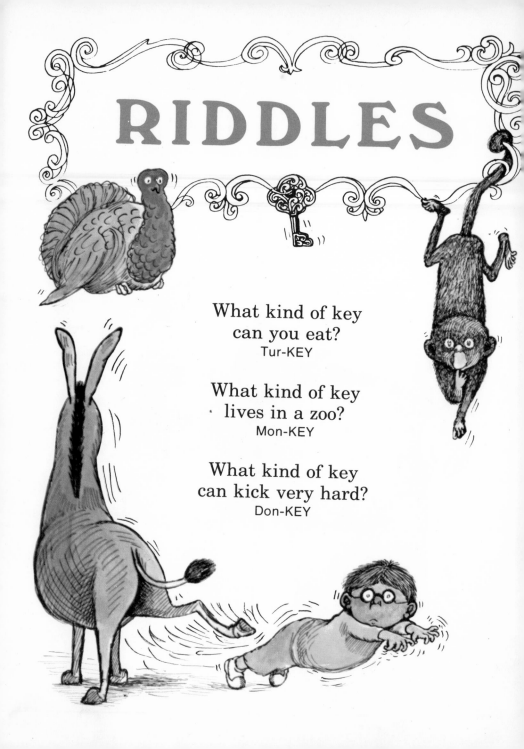

What kind of key
can you eat?
Tur-KEY

What kind of key
lives in a zoo?
Mon-KEY

What kind of key
can kick very hard?
Don-KEY

How long is a shoe?
1 foot long

What did the glove say to the hand?
"I've got you covered."

How did a belt break the law?
It held up some pants.

What can you make
that you can't see?
Noise

When is your mouth like the sky?
When a tooth comes out,
because there's SPACE

What day of the week is best for boys?
Sunday (SON-day)

What day of the week is lazy?
SAT-urday

What day of the week is a good cook?
Friday (FRY-day)

How do you know the elephant will stay
for a long time when he comes to visit?
He brings his trunk.

On which side does a bear have thick fur?
On the outside

What flying animal is always
found at a baseball game?
Bat

When a Cub Scout jumps into a lake,
what is the first thing he does?
Gets wet

When were you twins?
When you were two

You are my brother but I am not
your brother. Who am I?
Your sister

What letter is a bird?
J (Jay)

What letter can sting?
B (Bee)

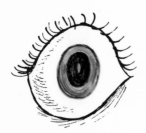

What letter is part of the face?
I (Eye)

What letter does not need glasses?
C (See)

10

Which animal
did not tell the truth?
Lion (lyin')

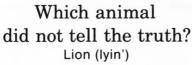

Which dog always knows what time it is?
Watch dog

Why did the little pig eat so much?
He was making a hog of himself.

What is a kitten after it is four days old?
Five days old

What number is not hungry?
8 (Ate)

What color is noisy?
YELL-ow

Which year can jump very high?
Leap year

How do we know the ocean is friendly?
It waves.

In what way are a bed, a lion,
and a river alike?
Each has springs.

Why did the big rope scold the little rope?
It was knotty (naughty).

What kind of snake is most like a penny?
COPPER-head

What fruit is on a nickel?
Date

Which coin does a skunk have?
Cent (scent)

Why does the mailman have a blue truck?
To carry the mail

What song did the frying pan sing?
"Home on the Range"

JOKES

Horse: "Your feet make me think of my dad."
Dog: "That's silly. Why would my feet make you think of your dad?"
Horse: "They're paws (pa's)."

Girl: "Are you going to take the bus home?"
Boy: "No. My mother would only make me take it back."

Sue: "What was the hardest thing about learning to roller skate?"
Ted: "The floor."

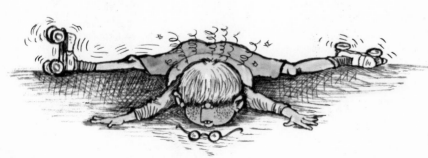

Jack: "Ron's mother won't let him keep
frogs at their house, so he found
some water and put them in."

Mother: "Oh, that's fine. Where did he
find the water?"

Jack: "In our bathtub."

Jill: "I have a dog."
Sam: "A bird dog?"
Jill: "No."
Sam: "A poodle?"
Jill: "No."
Sam: "What kind?"
Jill: "A hot dog!"

John: "What would you say if you saw
               a ghost?"
Sue: "Not a word. I'd just run!"

Little Ghost: "I'm going to sing with the
                               big ghosts today."
Very Little Ghost: "What are you going to sing?"
Little Ghost: "A-Haunting We Will Go."

Tim: "I don't like Sally. I don't want
               to go to her birthday party."

Mother: "You must go, Tim. Now, what would
               you like to give her?"

Tim: "Measles."

Bill: "I hit the nail with a hammer."
Father: "That's fine."
Bill: "No. It was my thumb nail."

Doctor: "How do you feel today?"
Girl: "With my hands, sir."

Lady: "Are you sleepy?"
Girl: "No. I'm Susan."

Said Father Goat to his son:
  "Stop butting in when I'm talking."

Said the boy to the match:
  "I'm going to strike you."

Said the little stream to the river:
  "You and your big mouth!"

Said Mother Moth to her children:
  "Eat your good wool dinner."

Teacher: "Where is milk stored?"
Girl: "In a cow."

Teacher: "Use the word BARREL
            in a sentence."
Jane: "Run or the BARREL bite you."

Teacher: "Johnny, use the word TACKLE in
            a sentence."
Johnny: "Anybody who sits on a TACKLE
            be sorry."

Pam: "Mother, the dog won't eat the
              candy I gave him."

Mother: "Well, get rid of the candy."

Pam: "I did. I gave it to Tommy."

Joe: "When do dogs have 12 legs?"

Sam: "I don't know. When do they have
          12 legs?"

Joe: "When there are 3 of them."

Boy: "I want a winter coat."
Clerk: "How long?"
Boy: "For the whole winter."

Lady: "Don't cry like that, little girl."
Girl: "Then how shall I cry?"

Jim: "I was on TV today."

Pat: "What fun! How long were you on?"

Jim: "Not very long. As soon as my mother saw me sitting there, she made me get off."

Kathy: "How did you get that bump on your head?"

Tom: "Diving."

Kathy: "Where were you diving?"

Tom: "In the bathtub."

Teacher: "What is the matter, Johnny?"
Johnny: "I itch."
Teacher: "What is making you itch?"
Johnny: "I went to a circus."
Teacher: "Now, Johnny, why would going to a circus make you itch?"
Johnny: "It was a flea circus."

Jill: "Can you spell 'House' with
2 letters?"
Mary: "No. How do you spell 'House'
with 2 letters?"
Jill: "TP (teepee)."

Baby Broom was cross and tired. Mother
    Broom held Baby Broom close and sang, "Go
    to Sweep, Baby. Go to Sweep."